2001
DECORATIVE CUTS
AND
ORNAMENTS

Edited by
Carol Belanger Grafton

DOVER PUBLICATIONS, INC., *New York*

Published in Canada by General Publishing Company, Ltd.,
30 Lesmill Road, Don Mills, Toronto, Ontario.
Published in the United Kingdom by Constable and Company,
Ltd.

2001 Decorative Cuts and Ornaments is a new work, first
published by Dover Publications, Inc., in 1988.

DOVER *Pictorial Archive* SERIES

Manufactured in the United States of America
Dover Publications, Inc., 31 East 2nd Street, Mineola, N.Y.
11501

Library of Congress Cataloging-in-Publication Data

2001 decorative cuts and ornaments / edited by Carol Belanger
    Grafton.
            p.   cm.
        ISBN 0-486-25612-X (pbk.)
        1. Type ornaments. 2. Printers' ornaments. 3. Print-
    ing—Specimens. 4. Vignettes. 5. Decoration and ornament.
    I. Grafton, Carol Belanger. II. Title: Two thousand one
    decorative cuts and ornaments. III. Title: Two thousand and
    one decorative cuts and ornaments.
    Z250.3.A16   1988
    686.2'24—dc19   87-32166
                                                        CIP

Publisher's Note

 The 2001 (actually over 2200) decorative cuts and ornaments in this collection exemplify the high artistic standards of nineteenth- and early twentieth-century illustrators, designers, and engravers. The cuts have been specially selected by graphic artist Carol Belanger Grafton for their usefulness to modern graphic artists, designers, and advertisers. They are all copyright-free.

The variety of this superb compendium is such as to suit almost any mood, style, or subject. While the cuts are too various to be described here in any detail, leafing through this volume will present the following types of images in, very approximately, the following arrangement (on the pages indicated):

General decorative designs (many incorporating flowers, fruit, and architectural features): 1–32
Objects (ranging from a fountain to a flag to a factory): 33–44
Human figures: 45–59
Food and drink: 60–61
Music and dance motifs: 62–65
Sports and recreational activities: 66–69
St. Nicholas and various emblems of Christmas: 70–72
Cherubs and angels: 73–77
Astrological signs: 78
Nautical and seashore motifs: 79
Modes of transportation: 80–81
Animals (real and fanciful): 82–89
End cuts ("finis"): 90–91

(The designs incorporate these motifs in various combinations as well, so if you don't find exactly what you want in one category, check others.)

The sources for this immensely varied collection include a multitude of nineteenth- and twentieth-century American and European publications, among them periodicals such as *The Century Magazine, Harper's Magazine, Simplicissimus*, and *The Studio*; printers' periodicals such as *The British Printer, The Inland Printer*, and *The Printing Art*; *L'Art pour tous, Dekorative Vorbilder, The Printers' International Specimen Exchange*, and other collections of ornamental designs, as well as various illustrated books; and typefounders' catalogues, printers' specimen leaflets, and various typographic ephemera.

1

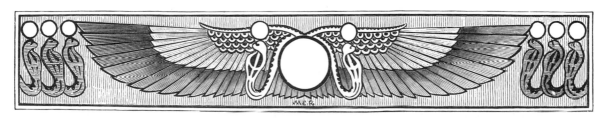

11

15

17

18

POST CARD

POST CARD

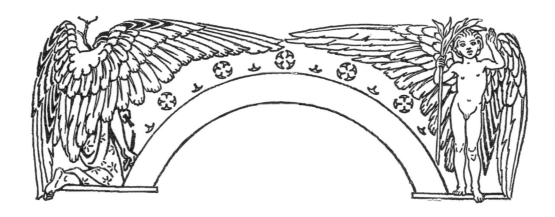

35

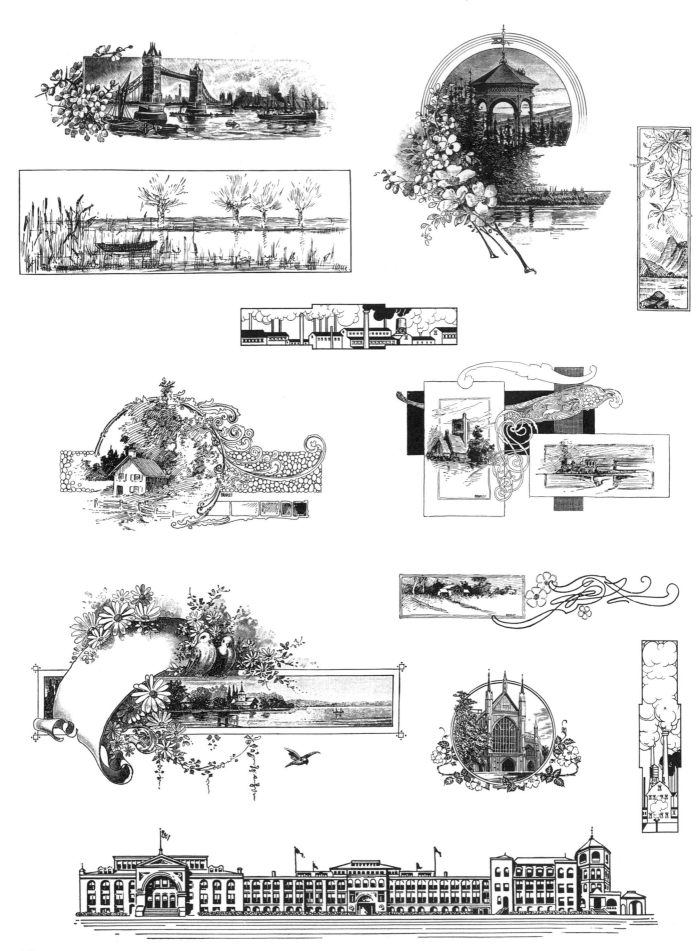

38

50

54

59

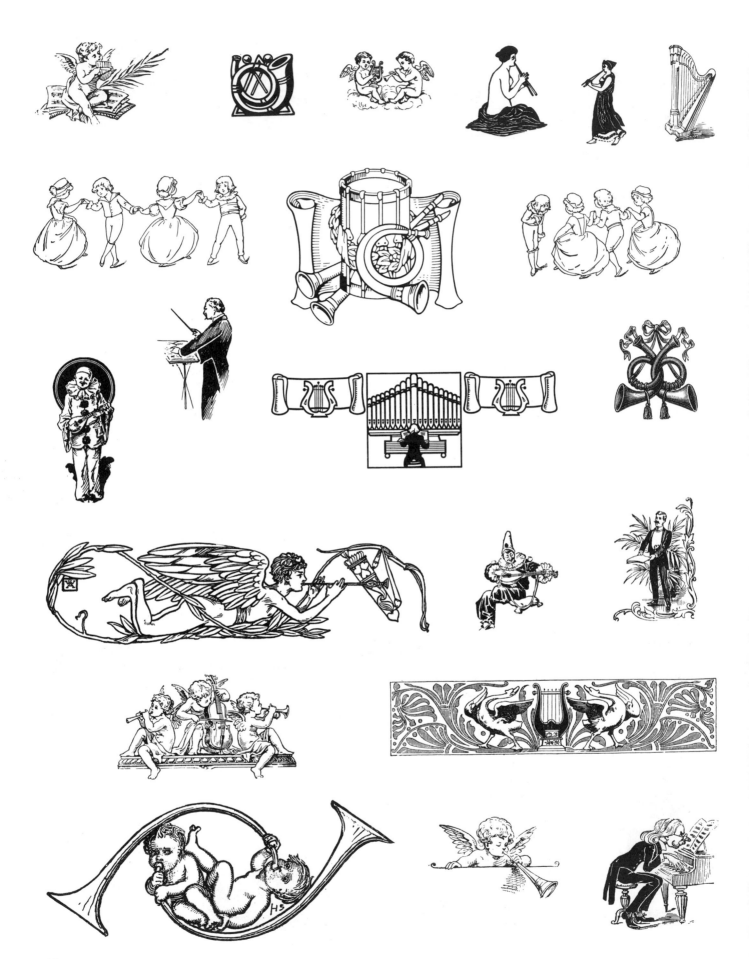

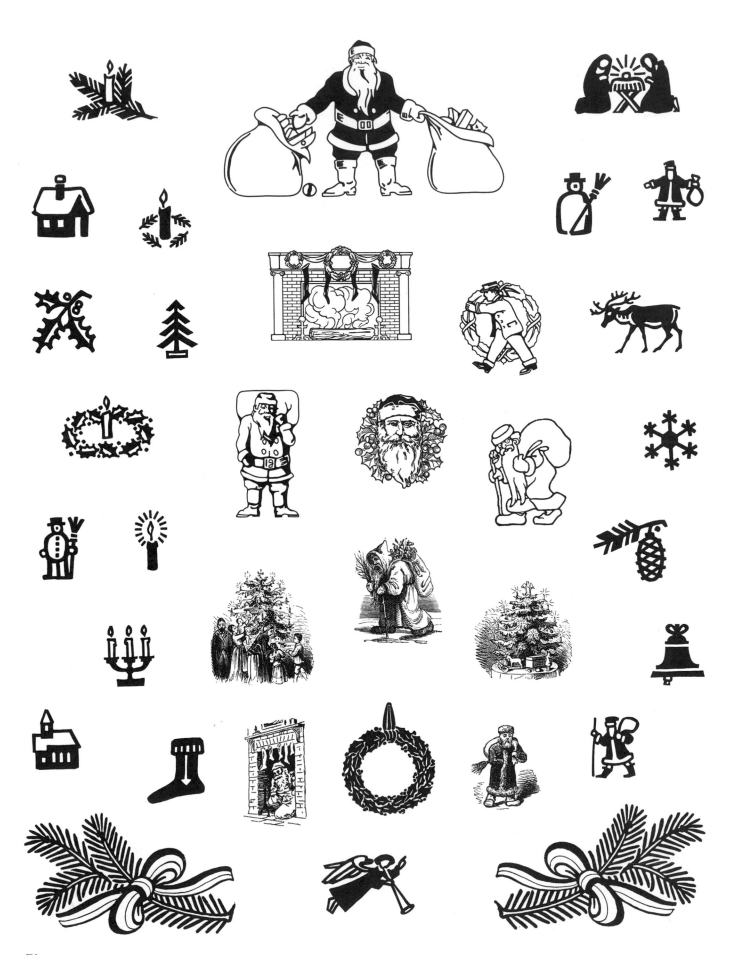

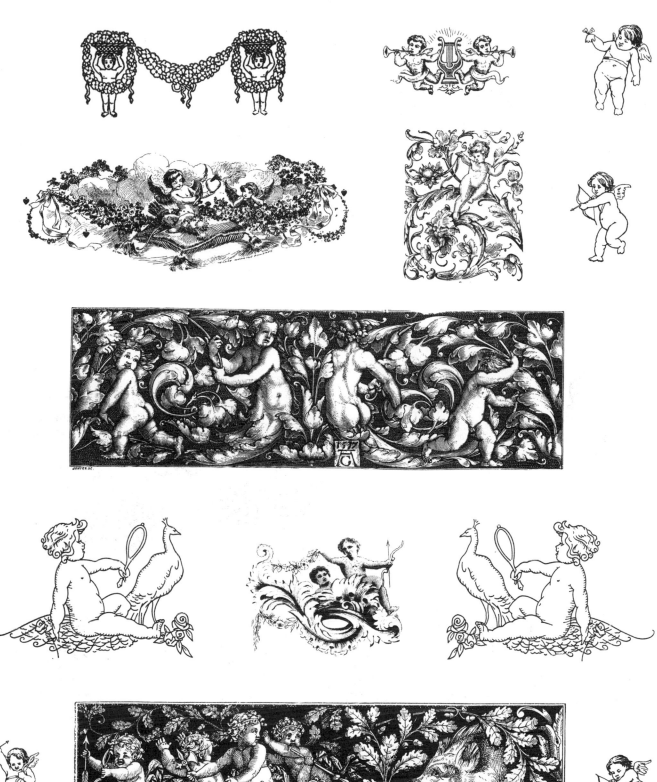

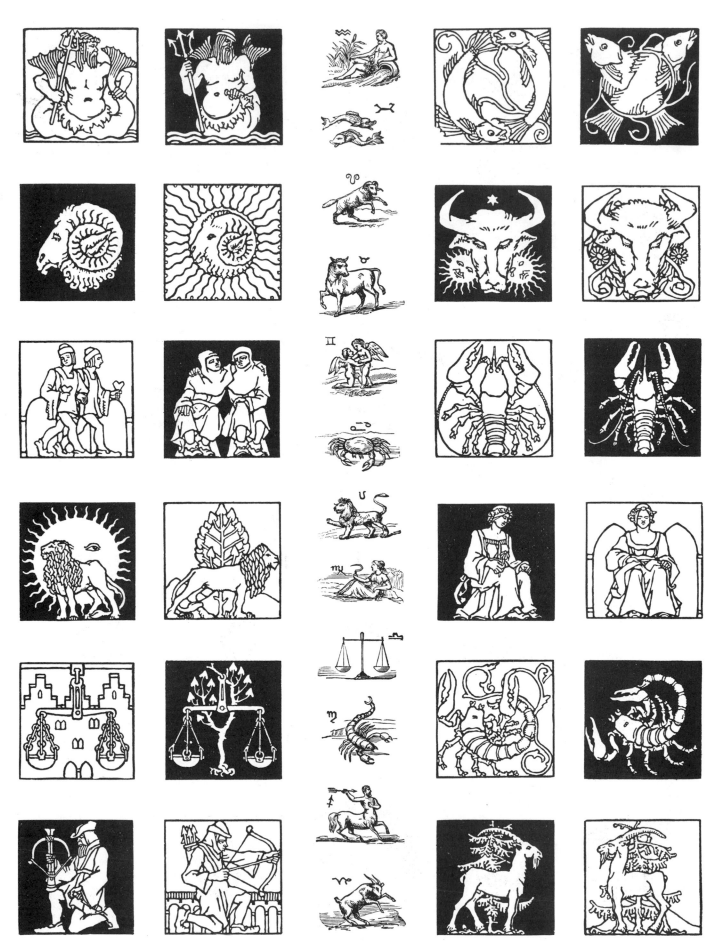

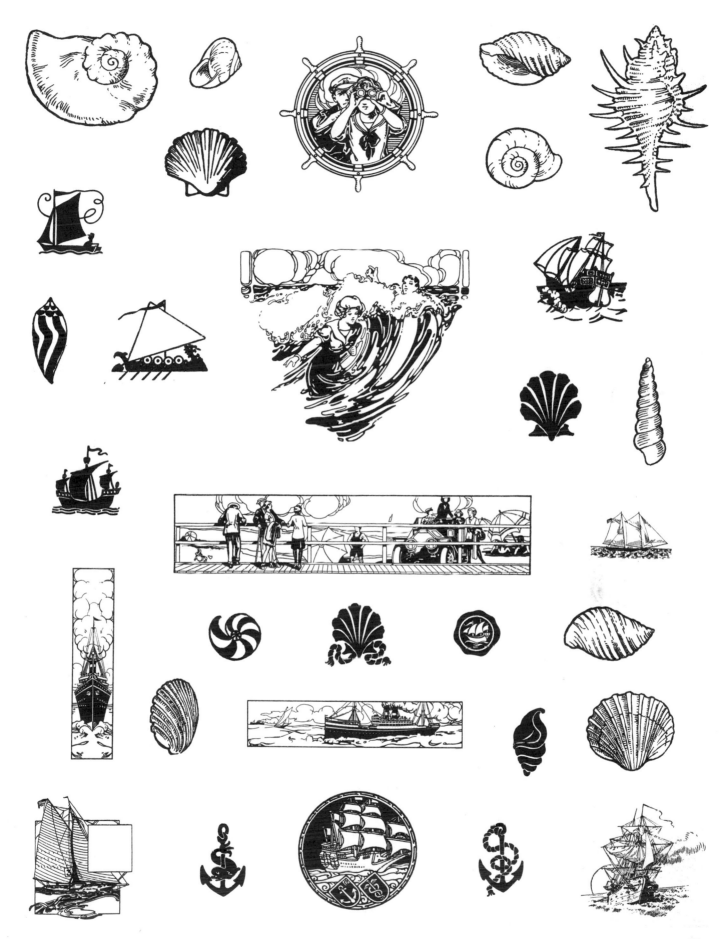

90